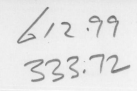
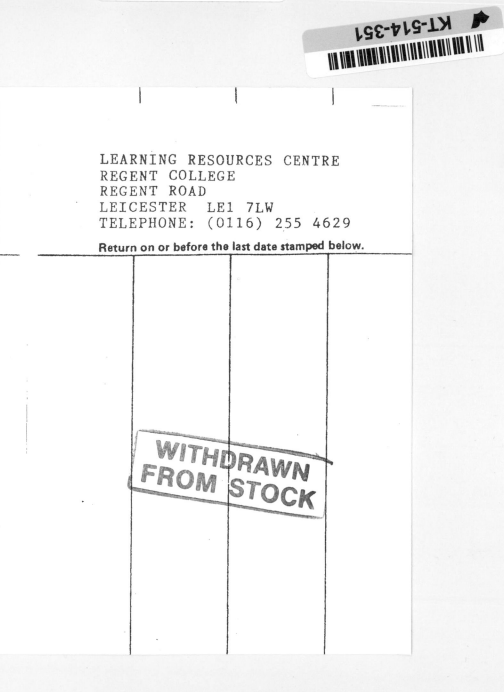

Working for our Future

Sustaining the Environment

Judith Anderson

In Association with Christian Aid

 We believe in life before death

FRANKLIN WATTS
LONDON·SYDNEY

First published in 2007 by
Franklin Watts
338 Euston Road
London NW1 3BH

Franklin Watts Australia
Level 17/207 Kent Street
Sydney NSW 2000
Copyright © Franklin Watts 2007

Editor: Jeremy Smith
Art director: Jonathan Hair
Design: Rita Storey

Produced in association with Christian Aid.

Franklin Watts would like to thank Christian Aid for their help with this title, in particular for allowing permission to use the information concerning Sara, Ayman, Gile, Dicynaba, Houlemata and Kardiata which is © Christian Aid.

Picture credits: Alamy: 7 all, 13b, 16t. Christian Aid/Amanda Farrant: 3cr, 9t, 15, 17b, 19b, 20t. Christian Aid/Elaine Duigenan: 3br, 17t, 24 all, 25t. Christian Aid/Sam Faulkner: 3bl, 6b, 11t, 14b, 21 all, 22t. Christian Aid/Simon Townsley: 3c, 12t, 27 all. Christain Aid/Sarah Malian: 23t. Corbis: 13t, 19t, 20b. istockphoto.com: 4-5 all, 6t, 10t, 12b, 14t, 18, 23b, 25b, 26b, 28 all, 29b. Millennium Villages Project: 22b. World Food Programme: 8 all, 9b, 10b, 11b.

Every attempt has been made to clear copyright. Should there by any inadvertent omission please apply to the publisher for rectification.

Dewey Classification 333.7s

ISBN: 978 0 7496 7350 5

Printed in China

Franklin Watts is a division of Hachette Children's Books, an Hachette Livre UK company.

The Millennium Development Goals

In 2000, government leaders agreed on eight goals to help build a better, fairer world in the 21st century. These goals include getting rid of extreme poverty, fighting child mortality and disease, promoting education, gender equality and maternal health and ensuring sustainable development.

The aim of this series is to look at the problems these goals address, show how they are being tackled at local level and relate them to the experiences of children around the world.

Contents

The Cast

In this book, follow the stories of these children and adults from around the world, all affected by environmental issues in different ways.

Nine-year-old **Ayman El' Asi** lives in the Gaza Strip, part of the Occupied Palestinian Territories in the Middle East. He works at a rubbish dump to earn money.

Ten-year-old **Gile Begum** lives in an area of Bangladesh which is badly affected by flooding.

Sara Amblo Rosel is eight years old. She lives in an area of rainforest in Bolivia, South America.

Dicynaba Mamadou Ba (above left) is eight years old. She lives in the village of Bewedji in Senegal with her aunt **Houleymata Diallo** (above centre) and her friend **Kardiata Ba** (above right).

Your environment

Look out of the window for a moment. What can you see? Some features are natural, such as rivers, clouds and hills. Other features are made by people, such as factories, farms and roads. What do you think of your environment? Do you like it?

Making an impact

Almost everything we do affects our environment. We build homes and work places, we grow food, we move about and burn fuel. Essential activities like cooking, washing and going to the toilet use water and power and create waste. In fact, it would be virtually impossible to live without making some kind of impact on our environment. Yet if the impact we make is too great, we can damage our environment.

We depend on our environment to grow crops to eat.

❝ I can't see much out of my window. There's too much pollution today! ❞

Selma (above), aged 11, Mexico City, Mexico.

❝ I can see the Eureka Tower. It's one of the tallest buildings in Melbourne. ❞

Millie, aged 10, Melbourne, Australia

▲ Every time we get on the bus to school we have an impact on our environment.

Global warming

Some activities have more of an impact than others. Burning fossil fuels produces gases known as carbon emissions, which many people believe have contributed towards the gradual warming of the Earth's atmosphere. Trees and other plants help to absorb some of these gases, but if we cut down too many trees or plants, or produce more carbon emissions than they can absorb, the atmosphere of the planet changes. This is called global warming, and it leads to higher temperatures, less overall rainfall and more stormy weather.

▲ We have to protect our environment if we want it to carry on providing food for us.

? **What impact do you have on your environment?**

The world's resources

Our planet has a limited amount of land, water, clean air, forests and other resources. Yet if people do not have access to these resources, they cannot eat well, be healthy and develop economically. Sustaining the environment is about using the world's resources sensibly so that poor people in particular are able to benefit from them both now and in the future.

A forest under threat

Around the world, rainforests are being chopped down by timber companies to make money or by farmers to clear land to put their animals on. Sara Amblo Rosel lives with her parents in the rainforest of Bolivia, the poorest country in South America. Her parents share an area of land with the rest of her community, but life became difficult when cattle ranchers tried to take their land and clear the forest where she lived to make room for their animals.

▲ Rainforests are disappearing at a rate of about 17 million hectares a year, an area larger than Switzerland.

" The cattle ranchers cut down the wood in our forest. They took over our land, the land we had worked on, often some of the best land. **"**

Sara's father Malaquia remembers what happened to their land:

6

Living in a desert

Dicynaba Mamadou Ba is eight years old. She lives in the village of Bewedji in Senegal with her aunt Houleymata Diallo, and her friend Kardiata Ba. The village lies far away from the river and is built in an area of desert. The nearest borehole (a hole drilled to supply water) is 7 km away, and it is shared by 29 other villages. The land they live on has become a desert because of erosion and because the people that live there have overused the resources around them.

Severine Flores, on behalf of Christian Aid, says:

It is very hot and dry in Senegal. Livestock, such as camels and cattle, often overgraze what little plant life grows.

" Here the reality of the desert is stark – whichever direction you look in, it reaches to the horizon. There is no evidence of water or of substantial vegetation. The land is very dry and dusty. "

? Which resources do the families of Sara and Dicynaba need most? Why?

The problem of water

Water is our most precious natural resource. We need it for drinking, cooking, washing and to make toilets flush. It is also essential for farming and industry. In fact, we cannot live without it. However, getting it isn't that easy for many people. Some people live in areas of low rainfall, or drought. Others only have access to water that is dirty or polluted.

▲ A teacher dishes up clean drinking water out of a huge metal pot at a school feeding programme in North Kordofan state, Sudan.

Unsafe water

People in developing countries often don't have access to pipes and taps that help to ensure a supply of clean water. They have to rely on water from open wells, lakes and rivers. This water is often polluted by animal or human waste, which spreads diseases like diarrhoea.

Not enough water

The areas of the world most seriously affected by drought are parts of Africa and South Asia. Four out of ten Africans don't have proper access to water. Their crops fail, their animals die and their livelihoods are devastated. Low rainfall isn't the only reason for the world's water shortage, however. Some people are simply using too much, causing rivers and underground reserves to run dry.

Some scientists have estimated that the amount of water leaking from taps in developed countries is enough to supply one billion people in developing countries.

◀ Stunted crops in Kora village, on the Dale district of Ethiopia.

Too much water!

In other parts of the world, flooding is a serious problem. The plains of Bangladesh are naturally prone to floods, but in recent years global warming has meant that water levels are rising and the flooding has become more severe. Flood water itself is not clean water. As well as causing terrible damage to homes and farms, it spreads disease and infects clean water supplies.

Gile lives in a district called Sumanganj in Bangladesh. During the 2004 floods she had to stay on the bed in her house for nearly two months to avoid the flood water.

" We were up to our knees in water in all the rooms. We were lucky we could still collect clean water from the tube well outside our house and we lifted up the latrine (toilet) by placing two concrete rings underneath it. "

Flood scenes in Indonesia, February 2006. Countries like Indonesia suffer from flooding on a regular basis.

? How would your life be affected if your home flooded?

Not enough land

The world is becoming more crowded. The population in many developing countries is rising, and cities are getting bigger and bigger as more people arrive in search of jobs and homes. However, many areas cannot cope with such rapid growth. Often it seems there is not enough food, water, land and shelter to go round. When this happens, the poorest people often lose out.

▲ Rush hour in Tokyo. Japan is one of the most heavily populated countries on earth.

Slums

A slum is an area of a city where poor people live in overcrowded conditions, often illegally. People live in crude, basic shacks made out of cheap materials such as corrugated iron. Access to clean water, toilets and electricity is extremely limited. In one slum area of Mumbai in India, over 5,000 people have to share one toilet. Pollution and disease spread rapidly in such conditions. Those who live there have little hope of raising themselves out of poverty.

Almost one in six of the world's population now lives in slums, and almost all of these are in developing countries. Kibera in Nairobi, Kenya, is one of the world's biggest slums. Over 700,000 people live there. ▶

Unfair treatment

The poorest people are often treated unfairly by the rest of society. Because slum dwellers are forced to live in illegal housing, they can be evicted and their homes destroyed without any kind of legal protection. Essential resources like clean water often cost more in slum areas, and the United Nations estimates that some poor people have to pay up to ten times more for their water than wealthier people.

Farmers in rural areas may also find their land is wanted by others. The Rosel family didn't know what to do when cattle ranchers tried to take their land. Sara's father says:

"It felt like they had more power than us. They had people with guns, they had money and lawyers. They weren't from here."

No rights

Many poor people don't know about their rights. This means that landowners and governments find it easier to discriminate against them and cheat them out of what they are entitled to by law. In areas such as Dafur in Sudan (left), many black Africans have had their land taken from them by the pro-Arab government.

◀ These people in the Kirindang camp in Darfur, Sudan, have had their homes seized by the government.

? How do you think Sara and her family felt when the cattle ranchers tried to take their land?

Too much waste

Wherever there are people, there is waste. Dirty water, sewage, paper and plastic, fumes from cars, chemicals from factories – sometimes it seems as if the world is one big waste bin. Some of it we can recycle, or re-use. Some of it will eventually rot, or decay. But much of it stays with us, causing problems for future generations.

❝ I come here every day. I am the only member of my family who works and I decided to do this to help them. **❞**

Ayman is nine years old. He lives near a rubbish dump in the northern Gaza Strip and goes there every day to collect plastic bottles that he sells to earn money for his family. The smell is terrible and Ayman's eyes have an infection caused by fumes from burning car rubbish.

The biggest producers

We don't all produce the same amount of waste. Developed countries consume more and therefore produce more waste, such as chemicals and plastic. However, they can also afford to develop and use cleaner types of fuel and invest in sophisticated recycling programmes. Developing countries tend to rely on the cheaper, most polluting types of fuel such as wood and coal.

War and services

Sometimes conflict and violence can also destroy people's services. When this happens, it is usually the poorer people who suffer most.

▲ Visible air pollution hangs in the air over Los Angeles, USA. Rich countries, such as the United States and China, cause far more pollution per person than poorer countries.

Climate change

One of the biggest threats to our environment comes from climate change. Increasing carbon and other greenhouse gases in the earth's atmosphere mean that the world is getting warmer and melting ice caps, causing water levels to rise and making weather unpredictable. These changes can have a devastating impact on whole communities. Crops and habitats are affected, and the homes of people living close to sea level are now increasingly under threat from flooding and loss of clean water. Once again, it is the poorest people who are least able to protect themselves against such disasters.

▲ Bangladeshi people inspect erosion damage left by the river Jamuna in Sariakandi, northwest of Dhaka. The area flooded in 2004.

People living in a village near Gile (left) have already seen their homes destroyed by rising river levels and the erosion of the river bank. Gile says:

❝ I have heard about global warming from the teacher at school. I've heard that snow in the mountains is melting and the sea water levels are rising so that our villages will be inundated (flooded). ❞

? Why are poorer people more likely to suffer from the effects of waste and pollution?

The need for change

More people, fewer resources, greater use of chemicals and fossil fuels and an ever-growing need for food, water and land have placed the environment under enormous pressure. This cannot continue without a devastating impact on many people around the world.

 This rainforest in Tasmania has been destroyed by logging companies.

A difficult problem

Every country needs to work to create new policies to protect vulnerable communities, to reduce the impact of pollution, waste and climate change, to conserve the natural environment and to improve access to resources so that clean water, food and land are available to more people in the future.

But sometimes it can be difficult to achieve one of these goals without destroying another. How can farmers grow more and better crops without using more harmful pesticides or cutting down more trees? How can developing countries grow without burning dangerous amounts of cheap fossil fuels?

Malaquia Rosel, Sara's father, says:

“ I am Bolivian, I am proud of my country, we have all the gifts of nature. But I don't understand why people are so poor. I want my children to have a stable home with land to work and live on. ”

Working together

Sustaining the environment is about governments and communities working together to find ways to allow everyone to share in the world's resources while at the same time making sure that they are properly protected and replenished.

" Bangladesh contributes less than one per cent of the world's total greenhouse gas emissions, but is expected to be one of the countries hardest hit by climate change. **"**

Christian Aid.

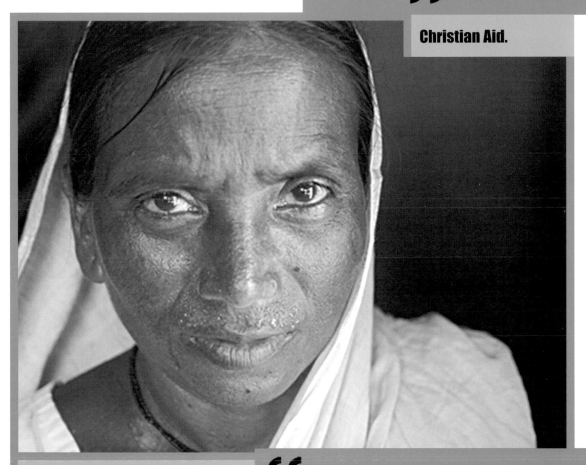

Sunita Ranidash is an older woman who lives near Gile in Bangladesh. She is aware of the damage caused to her country by rising temperatures.

" The floods have been getting worse bit by bit since I was a child. Each year the temperature seems to be increasing too. As the temperature rises, we are facing many new types of diseases and epidemics. **"**

 What could be done to reduce the amount of disease in Sunita and Gile's village?

The Millennium Development Goals

In the year 2000 the world's leaders met at the United Nations and agreed a set of eight goals that would help to make the world a better, fairer place in the 21st century. Goal seven is to ensure environmental sustainability, but all eight goals are closely linked to improving the lives of poorer people and giving everyone an equal chance.

Al Gore, US politician and environmental campaigner, says:

❝ We only have one Earth. And if we do not keep it healthy and safe every other gift we leave our children will be meaningless. **❞**

The Goals

Each goal has targets that need to be achieved by a specific date, and governments have been asked to make policies to ensure these targets are met. The targets for goal seven are as follows: reverse the loss of environmental resources; reduce by half the number of people without long-term access to safe drinking water; significantly improve the lives of at least 100 million slum dwellers.

THE EIGHT MILLENNIUM DEVELOPMENT GOALS

1 Get rid of extreme poverty and hunger

2 Primary education for all

3 Promote equal chances for girls and women

4 Reduce child mortality

5 Improve the health of mothers

6 Combat HIV/AIDS, malaria and other diseases

7 Ensure environmental sustainability

8 Address the special needs of developing countries, including debt and fair trade

Working together

Houleymata's land in Senegal has become a desert because of land erosion. She hopes they can work to change this.

Houleymata Diallo explains how her environment has been changed during her lifetime:

❝ We used to be able to cultivate this land. It was a good life. When I was young I couldn't see beyond a hundred metres in front of me, but as time has gone by, the trees have gone. There is erosion of the soil and now you can see 25 km. **❞**

Gile knows that environmental problems cause illness:

❝ There's lots of disease in this village. Things that make people ill are bad food, dust and polluted water. I want to be a doctor one day so that I can cure other people. **❞**

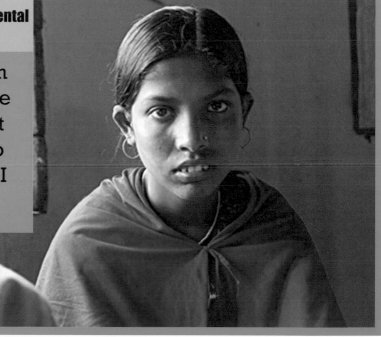

 Houleymata and Gile both have hopes for the future. What would help them realise their dreams?

Government action

All governments can make laws to control the type and amount of energy they use, the amount of waste they produce and to ensure fairer access to resources such as land and water. However, some governments pass stricter laws than others. All governments must work together to find ways to protect our planet and create a more sustainable environment for all.

▲ Fridges and freezers leak gases called CFCs (chlorofluorocarbons) into the atmosphere. Over the last ten years, governments around the world have cooperated to reduce the use of CFCs by 90 per cent.

Developed countries

The governments of developed countries can invest in more energy-efficient fuels and share this technology with developing countries. They can cancel the debts of poorer countries, so that these countries have more money to build schools, hospitals, water systems

and sustainable housing for a better quality of life. They can also agree to limit their own consumption of resources so that there is more for everyone else.

Developing countries

The governments of developing countries can educate people about more efficient farming practices, conserving water and growing crops that are more resistant to drought and floods. They can build more sustainable cities, with proper sanitation, water and energy supplies. They can also develop industries such as forestry and eco-tourism that combine economic growth with environmental protection.

President Alan Garcia of Peru has promised to provide drinking water to 2.5 million people by July 2009. The United Nations estimates that Peru could also reduce child deaths by 60 per cent if proper drains and sewers were built across the country.

❝ There is a battle for water going on in Peru. It's one of the country's main problems and it is our job to solve it. **❞**

The prime minister of Peru, Jorge del Castill (above left) speaks about his country's water shortages.

Gile lives in a tin shed house with straw walls inside. Her village is flooded every year and each time many homes are swept away. She needs help from her government.

❝ We could go to the two storey building in the market but you have to pay to be able to stay there. **❞**

 What might Gile's government do to help her?

Local solutions

Different communities have different needs. A city slum might need more toilets or better housing, while a remote village might need a new well or help with crops and animals. All over the world, charities, aid organisations and community groups are working with local people to find the best solutions for problems in their area.

Planning ahead

A charity called Friends in Village Development Bangladesh (FIVBD) has helped people in Gile's village by working with them to rebuild flood-damaged homes and farms and be better prepared against future flooding. FIVBD has also set up projects such as duck farms and vegetable gardens to make sure that villagers can increase their ability to cope with disasters by managing and profiting from their own supply of food.

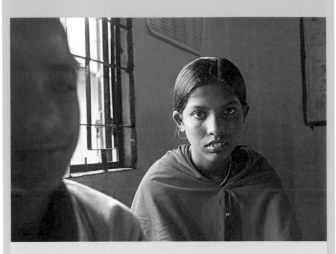

Already Gile has a clear idea of how to protect her family's home and food supply when the next flood comes.

“ I think to be better prepared for floods we should make a platform inside the house so we can store food and our school books there. Our house should be strong. We can use rope to tighten the bamboo poles and if we can raise the floor of the house then water won't come into the room. ”

A flood protection scheme using earth embankments and supporting poles in a village near to Gile's.

The sheep from CIPCA are a woolless kind that are better suited to living in the rainforest and produce good quality meat. Sara says:

> **"** I like it when the people from CIPCA come, they help me with the sheep. I help look after the sheep and I know which ones are ours because we cut their ears in a special shape. **"**

Land rights

The Centre for the Research and Training of Peasant Farmers (CIPCA) is a local organisation that provides training and support for small farmers in the part of Bolivia where Sara Amblo Rosel lives. When farms in the area were threatened by the cattle ranchers, CIPCA told them about their rights and helped them keep their land and their livelihoods. Sara's mother Edith says that because the CIPCA have advised them to keep cows on their land and grow crops, it is harder for the cattle ranchers to take it from them.

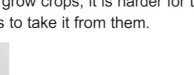

Sara says:

> **"** Before I ate only rice. Now I eat all these things we grow! **"**

A helping hand

CIPCA has also given sheep to local families for breeding and meat. It has given people seeds and shown them how to grow different kinds of crops that will provide them with more food to eat and to sell. Sara's family now also keeps sheep and hens and grow cocoa trees as well as bananas, mandarins and grapefruit.

? **Why do you think growing several different types of crops is better for Sara and her family?**

People who help

All sorts of people are working to ensure a more sustainable environment around the world today. Scientists try to reduce the impact of climate change. Aid managers raise money and organise the distribution of resources. Agricultural specialists show people how to farm more productively and local people get involved in community projects such as laying water pipes and recycling waste.

Carmiña prepares food with Sara's parents. She says:

❝ I value the relationship I have built up with the community leaders. We can speak frankly [honestly] with each other and we respect each other. **❞**

Managers

Carmiña Garcia is the director of the CIPCA office in the area of Bolivia where Sara lives. At first some people doubted whether she could do a good job because she is a young woman. However, she wanted to help the local farmers and showed them that together they could stand up to the cattle ranchers and make their voices heard.

Scientists

Dr Cheryl Palm is an American scientist working for the Millennium Villages Project which investigates ways in which the Millennium Development Goals can become a reality in villages across Africa.

Dr Cheryl Palm talks about her work in Africa.

❝ I see these projects in Africa as an exciting opportunity for experts to apply science to problems in developing countries. **❞**

Volunteers

Gul Allam Mohammedi lives in Kazugizouri village in a very dry and remote part of Afghanistan. Obtaining clean fresh water has always been a problem for everyone in his village, so when an organisation called the Agency for Humanitarian and Development Assistance in Afghanistan (AHDAA) offered to work together with local volunteers to lay new water pipes Gul was keen to get involved.

Gul Allam Mohammedi talks about working with AHDAA:

> ❝ I volunteered to help dig the pipeline for five months. Many of us volunteered because we were so thirsty - so thirsty for clean water. Clean water is the most important thing. ❞

Planners

Dr Deborah Brosnan is president of the Sustainable Ecosystems Institute and works with local communities affected by the Asian tsunami disaster in 2004. She says that communities must regain their self-sufficiency. Dr Brosnan and her company have pledged to help them rebuild their lives and to help them restore and protect the coral reef they depend on for tourism and diving.

◄ **Many communities depend on their natural resources such as coral reefs to attract tourists.**

? Have you ever tried to help someone who is having problems? How did it make you feel?

23

A sustainable future

A sustainable future means making the most of existing resources such as water, soil, oceans and forests without wasting them, polluting them or destroying them. In some of the poorest parts of the world, villagers are being taught how to make the most of the scarce resources around them.

Energy-saving stoves

In the past, people in Dicynaba's village have had to travel long distances to find fuel to build fires, and these fires were also very dangerous. Christian Aid have worked with the organisation Union par la Solidarité et l'Entraide (USE) to help villagers create their own energy-saving stoves out of natural materials. These have helped the local people save wood, and given them more time to devote to other things.

Dicynaba (left) describes how the new energy saving stoves (above) have changed the villagers' lives:

" Before we had the stove, you would have seen most of the houses around here burnt from fires because the wind would blow the fire into them. Also it's good to save wood and not collecting so much is a lot less tiring. "

Using resources

USE has taught people in the village of Bewedji to make better use of the natural resources around them. They have been shown how to look after trees and saplings and how to plant trees. They have also been encouraged to make better use of traditional trees around them, such as the jujube.

Mamadou Diop, USE's executive secretary says:

❝ Our role is to educate the community, preserve the environment and find things people can do to make a difference. That's why we have the training seminars to learn how to look after seeds and saplings and to plant trees. We look at how to plant new trees, exotic species and how to nurture them. **❞**

The jujube tree

In Bewedji, local trees such as the jujube were not thought to be of any use to villagers. Then it was discovered that traders in places like Dakar were drying the fruits and selling them. They were getting four times the price these fruits were sold for at the local market. So the growers in Dicynaba's village got organised and started working together to get a better price.

◀ **A jujube tree growing in Senegal.**

? **Why is it so important for Dicynaba and Mamadou to pass on the things they have learned?**

Sustainable cities

Sara, Gile, Ayman, Dicynaba, Houleymata and Kardiata are all working hard to build a better future for themselves by growing different types of food and taking steps to conserve resources. But what about people in cities? They need a sustainable environment, too.

Managing waste

Cities need good drains, clean water and proper toilets.Without these facilities the people who live there risk getting serious diseases and infections. David Kuria is the manager of a project to build toilet blocks in the Kibera slum in Nairobi, Kenya.

Renewable energy

Cities use a lot of energy. Most countries still rely heavily on non-renewable energy sources such as oil and coal, but these resources produce harmful waste and cannot be replaced once they have been used up. Now more and more people are beginning to use renewable energy sources such as solar power, which cause no damage to the environment.

David Kuria says:

" Toilets were a key priority. The waste will be collected in special digesters that produce a useful gas called methane that can be used for fuel. And a committee of local people will work together make sure that the toilets stay unblocked and clean. "

◀ **This house is part of an urban renewal project in the city of Leicester in the UK. Solar panels have been installed on the roofs of over 50 houses in the area, enabling people to use energy from the sun without harming the world around them.**

What future for Ayman?

Remember the story of Ayman, who works at a big rubbish dump in Gaza? He relies on other people's waste to earn a living. But the rubbish dump is full of dead animals and burning rubbish. Mosquitoes swarm everywhere. It is bad, very bad for the environment, and very bad for Ayman's health. If he keeps on working at the dump he might damage his lungs or catch a disease such as malaria.

" When I was six my father told me I had to start collecting plastic. When I was seven I had an accident collecting the plastic and I hurt my leg. When I grow up, I want to be an engineer and work in a factory. I want to stop collecting plastic bottles. "

Governments, city councils and local communities still have a long way to go if people like Ayman are to enjoy a sustainable future.

Ayman doesn't want to work on a rubbish dump all his life.

 How can Ayman be helped towards a better future for himself and his family?

Action you can take

We can all help to build a more sustainable environment, whether we are taking part in activities to look after our own communities, or working to bring about change for people in other countries. And don't forget that the things we do where we live often have an impact on the rest of the world.

Recycling helps to reduce the amount of waste we generate.

Reduce, re-use, recycle

Encourage everyone in your family or class at school to reduce the amount of packaging they use, re-use what they can and recycle other types of waste, such as plastic, textiles, glass and paper by taking them to a recycling depot. Rubbish that is not reduced, re-used or recycled is either burnt or buried in the ground. Both these methods pollute the environment.

Save water

Hold a water-awareness assembly and act out a small play to show how your audience can save water. Show them how much water is wasted when a tap is left running while you brush your teeth (about five litres!). Then talk about how someone in a developing country might use that water. People in developed countries use over 13 times more water each day than the average person in Africa.

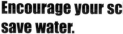

Encourage your school friends to save water.

We believe in life before death

▲ The official logo of the charity Christian Aid, who help poor children around the world, whatever their religion.

Support a charity

Many charities and aid organisations such as Wateraid are working to raise money, send resources, train advisers and campaign for the rights of poorer people in developing countries. Choose a suitable charity and contact them for suggestions about how you can raise awareness and raise money for things like water pumps, toilets, seeds and trees for people whose lives may depend on them.

Cut down on carbon!

Do you get to school by car? Try walking or cycling or, if you live too far away, see if there is anyone you can share lifts with. Planting a tree is another way to reduce the amount of carbon in the atmosphere because the leaves absorb it and use it to grow.

Make your voice heard

If you want to see your country take effective action on things like climate change and fairer access to resources, write to your government. Remind them about the Millennium Development Goals to which they have agreed and ask them what they are doing to achieve the targets for sustaining the environment.

◄ Reduce your carbon emissions by cycling to school rather than travelling by car.

? If you could meet Ayman, Sara, Gile, Dicynaba or Houleymata, what would you like to say to them?

Glossary

Carbon emissions the waste gases produced by burning fossil fuels.

Developing countries poorer countries.

Diarrhoea a stomach bug, often caused by poor hygiene.

Drought severe water shortage; lack of rain.

Environment the world around us.

Environmental pollution waste that harms the environment.

Environmental sustainability ensuring that there are enough natural resources for all, now and in the future.

Epidemic when disease spreads very quickly from one person to another.

Erosion the process by which the surface of the earth is worn away by the action of water, winds, waves and other weather.

Evicted to be made homeless.

Fossil fuels gas, coal and oil are fossil fuels - they are found beneath the earth's surface. Once they are used up they cannot be replaced.

Global warming a change in our planet's atmosphere which affects the climate. The effects include increased drought and flooding.

Millennium Development Goals (MDGs) 8 goals agreed by world leaders in the year 2000 with the aim of eradicating poverty and disease and promoting the rights of disadvantaged people.

Natural resources anything occurring naturally in our environment which we use in some way.

Pesticides chemicals designed to kill insects.

Renewable energy any energy source that will not run out (e.g solar power)

Self-sufficiency not dependent on others.

Solar power energy from the sun.

United Nations (UN) an organisation of countries from all around the world with the aim of promoting peace, development and human rights.

Find out more

Useful websites

www.millenniumcampaign.org
Click on "Goal 7" to find the latest news, facts and statistics as well as information about what you can do to help bring about sustainable development and fair access to the world's natural resources.

www.cyberschoolbus.un.org/mdgs
This site introduces all eight Millennium Development Goals with facts, photos and video clips to illustrate each one.

Send your story or poem about how any of the issues in this book have affected you to addyourvoice@unorg and view stories from other children on the link above (go to "Add your voice").

Note to parents and teachers:
Every effort has been made by the Publishers to ensure that these websites are suitable for children, that they are of the highest educational value, and that they contain no inappropriate or offensive material. However, because of the nature of the Internet, it is impossible to guarantee that the contents of these sites will not be altered. We strongly advise that Internet access is supervised by a responsible adult.

---

www.millenniumcampaign.org
For children aged 11 and over. Go to click on "Who's Doing What" (top of page), then "Youth" and download the Youth Action Guide.

www.wateraid.org.uk
Click on "Learn Zone", then "Games" for some great interactive games that allow you to play a role in solving some of the world's water problems.

Christian Aid websites

Christian Aid contributed all of the real-life stories in this book (the accounts of Sara, Ayman, Gile, Dicynaba, Houleymata and Kardiata). You can find out more about this organisation by following the links below:

www.christian-aid.org.uk
The main site for the charity Christian Aid, who help disadvantaged children and adults all over the world, regardless of their religion.

www.globalgang.org.uk
Christian Aid's website for kids with games, news and stories from around the world.

Index